# Asian Crafts

# Asian Crafts

## Judith Hoffman Corwin

FRANKLIN WATTS
New York/London/Toronto/Sydney

*Also by Judith Hoffman Corwin*

AFRICAN CRAFTS
COLONIAL AMERICAN CRAFTS: THE HOME
COLONIAL AMERICAN CRAFTS: THE SCHOOL
COLONIAL AMERICAN CRAFTS: THE VILLAGE
LATIN AMERICAN AND CARIBBEAN CRAFTS
PAPERCRAFTS

For Jules Arthur and Oliver Jamie

Library of Congress Cataloging-in-Publication Data

Corwin, Judith Hoffman.
    Asian crafts / Judith Hoffman Corwin.
        p.   cm.
    Includes index.
    Summary: Step-by-step instructions for making both ancient and
    modern crafts, toys, and foods from various countries on the Asian
    continent and from Japan.
    ISBN 0-531-11013-3
    1. Handicraft—Asia—Juvenile literature.   2. Toy making—Juvenile
    literature.   [1. Handicraft—Asia.   2. Toy making.   3. Cookery.
    4. Asia—Social life and customs.]   I. Title.
    TT160.C69   1991
    745.5—dc20
                                        91-13500
                                           CIP
                                            AC

# Contents

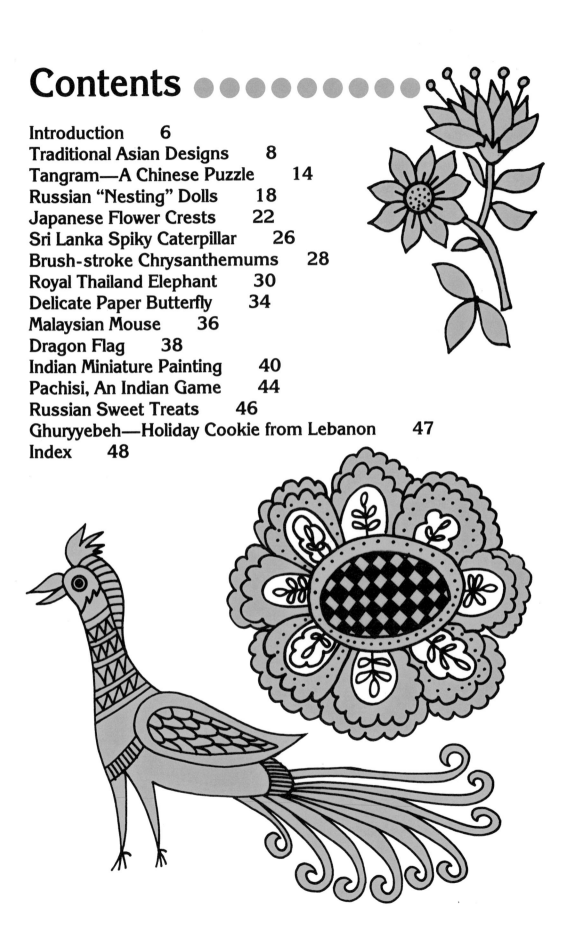

# Introduction ●●●●●●●●●●●

Asia is the largest of the five continents, both in area and in population. Its teeming masses and vast spaces encompass the widest diversity on earth.

In this book, you will learn how to make things in the style of both ancient and modern Asia, using materials that can be found mostly in your home. The projects given will help you experience something of each of the regions of this diverse continent: East Asia (China and Japan), Southeast Asia (Thailand and Malaysia), South Asia (India and Sri Lanka), Western Asia (Turkey and Lebanon), Central Asia (Afghanistan and Bhutan), and Northern Asia (Soviet Union). Early Asian artisans made large ceramic horses, beautifully decorated manuscripts, and treasures in gold and silver. They built palaces and temples, embroidered lovely ceremonial robes, carved ivory statues, and developed calligraphy into a high art with brush and ink.

Through art, we can enrich both our understanding of and respect for Asian people and their culture. By making projects inspired by Asian objects, crafts, and food, ordinary everyday materials can be messengers of this faraway continent.

The crafts of both ancient and modern Asia are important because they have produced functional, decorative, and expressive objects. Craft techniques were often passed on from father to son and mother to daughter so that they would remain alive. Today they are a true link to a cultural past and heritage.

This book is filled with ideas, information, folklore, and recipes from the world of Asia. They help to show that crafts know no boundaries— they are a basic human artistic expression. After all, there is only one world.

By following the clear and simple instructions included, you will be able to make many beautiful things. Explore and appreciate how Asian artists create designs in their own special way to capture the unique spirit of their continent. You will also want to experiment and create your very own projects or work on one with a friend.

7

# Traditional Asian Designs ●●●

On the next few pages, you will see a wide variety of traditional Asian designs. There are simple, abstract, and geometric ones. There are also animal designs to choose from—water buffalo, walrus, camel, gibbon ape, cobra, heron, crane, firebird, goldfish, cricket, panda, polar bear, and Arctic fox.

The designs can be used on stationery, greeting cards, wrapping paper, pictures, and T-shirts. You can paint on fabric, make a long scroll, cut designs out of paper and make a collage, or make up a story and illustrate it with designs from different countries. Just use your imagination. These wonderful designs can serve as inspiration for your own original drawings. You can have fun drawing them larger or smaller and changing them as you like. To begin, all you need is a pencil and a piece of paper.

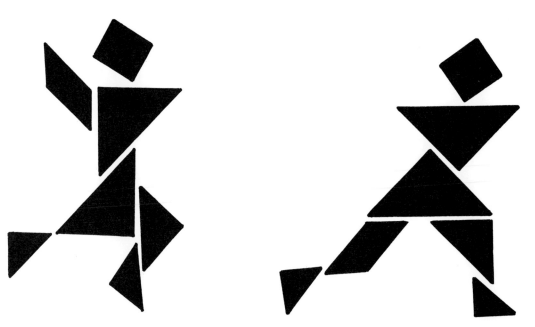

# Tangram—A Chinese Puzzle

Tangram is a nineteenth-century Chinese puzzle game that later spread around the world. The tangram is a 4″ square that has been cut into seven pieces, or tans. The object of the game is to invent an animal or other figure, shape, or design using all of the seven pieces. Striking examples of silhouettes can be made with this puzzle. There are over 1,500 possible solutions. Use your imagination and sense of humor to invent things. Look at the objects around you and in books and magazines, and try to simplify and make their shapes using the seven tans. After you play with the puzzle for awhile, you will begin to look at ordinary things in a new way. The only rules in tangram are that all seven pieces must be used in making a design, and none of the pieces may overlap. Before you begin, study the examples given: people running, two rabbits, a cat and dog, sailboat, and barn and bird.

## HERE'S WHAT YOU WILL NEED:

tracing paper
No. 2 soft lead pencil
teaspoon
4″ square of white oaktag
scissors

## HERE'S HOW TO DO IT:

**1.**   Use the pencil to trace the pattern for the tangram onto the tracing paper.

**2.**   Place the pencil-marked side of the tracing paper on top of the 4″ square of oaktag. Using the teaspoon, rub firmly along the pencil lines until the pattern is transferred.

**3.**   Cut along the pencil lines. You will have all seven pieces of the tangram ready to use. After you have become an expert with one seven-piece puzzle, you can try making another tangram so you can make more elaborate shapes.

# Russian "Nesting" Dolls ● ● ●

The real Russian "nesting" dolls are wooden with brightly painted faces and decorations. The largest ones have fifteen dolls inside them. You will be making four "nesting" dolls to fit neatly into each other. They are fun to line up in a row or to store one inside the other.

## HERE'S WHAT YOU WILL NEED:

1 can (like a coffee can) that is 4″ across the top and 5½″ high
1 can (like a peach can) that is 3″ across the top and 4⅜″ high
1 sheet white paper (like typing or computer paper)
1 can (like a frozen juice can) that is 2⅛″ across the top and 3¾″ high
wooden clothespin (the kind that has the rounded top); cut the bottom half off
tracing paper, No. 2 soft lead pencil, teaspoon
black fine-line felt-tip marker, tape
pink, yellow, orange, red, blue, and green colored markers

## HERE'S HOW TO DO IT:

**1.** Each can must be empty and clean and still have one lid remaining. This will be the top of the doll's head.

**2.** For each of the cans, you will need to cut a strip of paper the height of the can and long enough to go around the can, allowing for a 1″ overlap. You will be making the designs for each doll on the center of each of these strips.

**3.** Beginning with the largest doll, place a piece of tracing paper over the design given. Draw over the design with the pencil. Now place the pencil-marked side of the tracing paper on top of the center of the strip of paper for the largest doll. Using the teaspoon, rub firmly along the pencil lines until the design is transferred. Go over the pencil lines with the black fine-line felt-tip marker. Color in the cheeks with the pink marker, and color the rest of the designs as you like with the other markers. Repeat for the medium and small dolls.

● ● ● ● ● ● ● ● ● ● ● ● ● ● ● ● ●

**4.** Now you will be taping the finished strips to the proper cans. First tape one edge to the can from the top to the bottom, and then overlap the other edge of the paper, securing it with another piece of tape.

**5.** For the tiniest doll, use the black fine-line felt-tip marker to draw her face and decoration right onto the clothespin. Color in her cheeks with the pink marker and the rest of the designs as you like. Now your nesting dolls are ready for you to try out!

CUT →

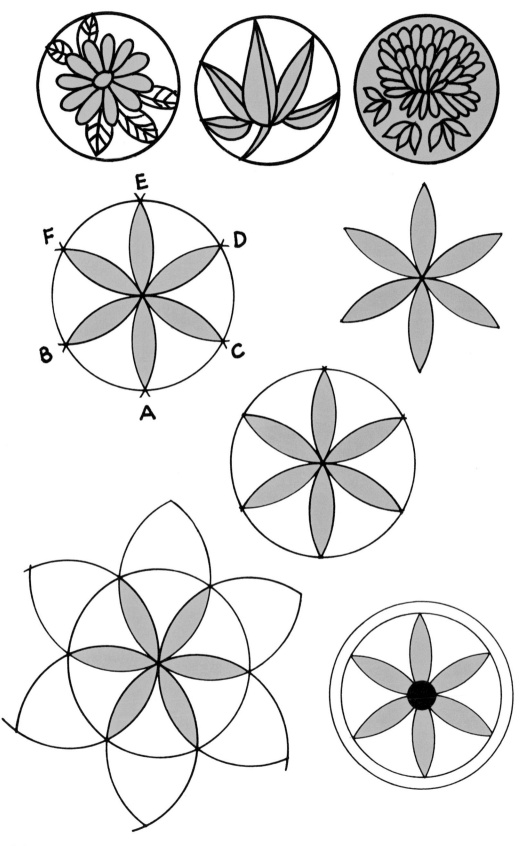

E

F D

B C

A

# Japanese Flower Crests ●●●●

These flower crest designs are super-easy to make with a compass. It's fun to experiment once you have mastered the basic flower. Traditionally, they are drawn in black and white and decorate ceremonial robes. You can find lots of wonderful uses for them. Create your own family crest and make stationery for yourself. Using the compass is a fast way to make bold, beautiful designs.

## HERE'S WHAT YOU WILL NEED:

white paper
compass with pencil point
black fine-line felt-tip marker
eraser

## HERE'S HOW TO DO IT:

**1.** Begin by opening the compass up 1″ wide. This will make a 2″ circle. Place the compass point in the center of the paper and draw a circle.

**2.** Place the point of the compass on point A and draw a curve from point B to point C. Check the illustration.

**3.** Now continue to make the flower by putting the compass point on point C and drawing a curve from point A to point D. Put the compass on point D and draw a curve from point C to point E. Put the compass point on point E and draw a curve from point D to point F. To complete the flower, put the compass point on point F and draw a curve from point E to point B. Experiment with drawing this and explore the other designs shown. You will quickly be able to make all of them.

**4.** After you have drawn your compass flowers, go over the pencil lines with the black marker and fill in the different areas to get interesting results and variations.

# Sri Lanka Spiky Caterpillar ●●

This little creature is at home in the jungle of Sri Lanka. It can be made to wriggle or bend. The edges are cut in spiky patterns, and it has a bold pattern along its back. It can be glued to a real leaf to make it feel cozy.

## HERE'S WHAT YOU WILL NEED:

8½″ × 11″ sheet of white paper
pointed scissors
black fine-line felt-tip marker

## HERE'S HOW TO DO IT:

**1.** With the point of the scissors, gently—without cutting through— mark a curvy line about 6″ long, as shown.

**2.** Cut out the outline of the caterpillar, about ½″ above and below each side of the curvy line.

**3.** Cut out a head, neck, four legs, and a tail, as shown. Cut spiky edges along its back. As you are working, look at the illustration. With the marker, draw in the eye and the decorations on the caterpillar's back.

# Brush-stroke Chrysanthemums ●●●●●●●

Both the Chinese and the Japanese cultures use the paintbrush to create the beautiful characters that make up their languages and to make expressive paintings. Here we will be making a chrysanthemum and a "good luck" symbol called "the double happiness." You can use these to decorate greeting cards, wrapping paper, or notecards or to make your own little painting.

## HERE'S WHAT YOU WILL NEED:

white paper
black ink
paintbrush that comes to a point

## HERE'S HOW TO DO IT:

Dip the paintbrush into the ink and begin to experiment with how it feels to hold the brush. Make a few strokes with it. Begin to follow the illustrations in order. You will be able to make the pretty chrysanthemum and the character.

# Royal Thailand Elephant ● ● ●

A very proud prince and princess are riding high on this mighty royal elephant, which is chasing a royal tiger. The elephant has long been a revered and popular animal in Thailand. Elephants appear in manuscripts, paintings, ceramics, and fabric designs. Legends are written about them. They are thought to be loyal, lovable, intelligent, and strong. In Thailand, as well as in other Asian countries, elephants travel in grand processions carrying members of the royal family. The elephants in these processions are decorated with richly painted patterns, gold, silver, and precious stones.

## HERE'S WHAT YOU WILL NEED:

$8^1/_2'' \times 11''$ piece of smooth-finish watercolor paper
No. 2 soft lead pencil, tracing paper, teaspoon
scissors, tape
permanent black fine-line felt-tip marker
paintbrush, watercolors
gold paint or marker
$1'' \times 5''$ strip of oak tag, for elephant's support
$1'' \times 2''$ strip of oak tag, for tiger's support

## HERE'S HOW TO DO IT:

**1.** Use the pencil to trace the elephant, prince, princess, and tiger onto the tracing paper.

**2.** Place the pencil-marked side of the tracing paper on top of the watercolor paper. Use the teaspoon to rub firmly along the pencil lines until all of the illustrations are transferred onto the watercolor paper.

**3.** Draw over all of these pencil lines with the black fine-line felt-tip marker.

**4.** Using the watercolors, paint everything in as you like. Remember that bright colors would be used in royal processions. Add extra patterns on the finished watercolors with the gold paint. Make small dots on the clothes of the prince and princess, on the elephant's blanket, and on the tiger's collar.

**5.** Cut out each figure from the watercolor paper. Make the two slits on the elephant, as shown. The prince and the princess have tabs on the bottom of them that will fit into the elephant. This will allow them to ride on the elephant.

**6.** Tape the oak tag supports to the back of the elephant and the tiger so that they will stand up.

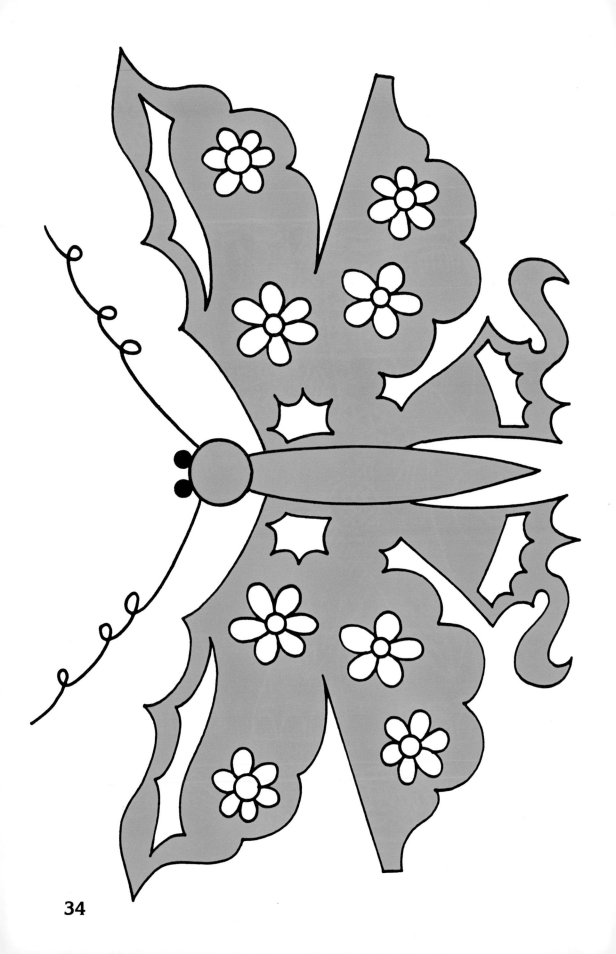

# Delicate Paper Butterfly ●●●●

A butterfly, as lovely and delicate as a real one, can be cut out of paper. The Asian art form of paper cutting creates designs that can be used to trim a special present for a friend, or to hang from the ceiling on a string, or to tape to a window so the sun can shine through its wings.

## HERE'S WHAT YOU WILL NEED:

$8^1/2'' \times 11''$ piece of white paper, folded in half
No. 2 soft lead pencil, tracing paper, teaspoon
sharp scissors, $8^1/2'' \times 11''$ piece of white typing paper
glue, black felt-tip marker
needle, white sewing thread, tape

## HERE'S HOW TO DO IT:

**1.** Use the pencil to trace the butterfly design onto the tracing paper.

**2.** Place the pencil-marked side of the tracing paper on top of the folded white paper. Using a teaspoon, rub firmly along the pencil lines until the design is transferred.

**3.** Working from the center of the design toward the outside, and using sharp scissors very carefully, cut away the colored areas of the design. When the inside cuts are complete, cut around the outside shape of the butterfly.

**4.** For the antennae, cut two $^1/8'' \times 4''$ strips of paper. Roll half of each strip in a tight coil and then release to form a curl. Glue to the butterfly's head. Make two tiny eyes with the black felt-tip marker. If you want to hang the butterfly from the ceiling, thread the needle with a 36" piece of thread. Put the thread through the tip of the butterfly's head and secure with a knot.

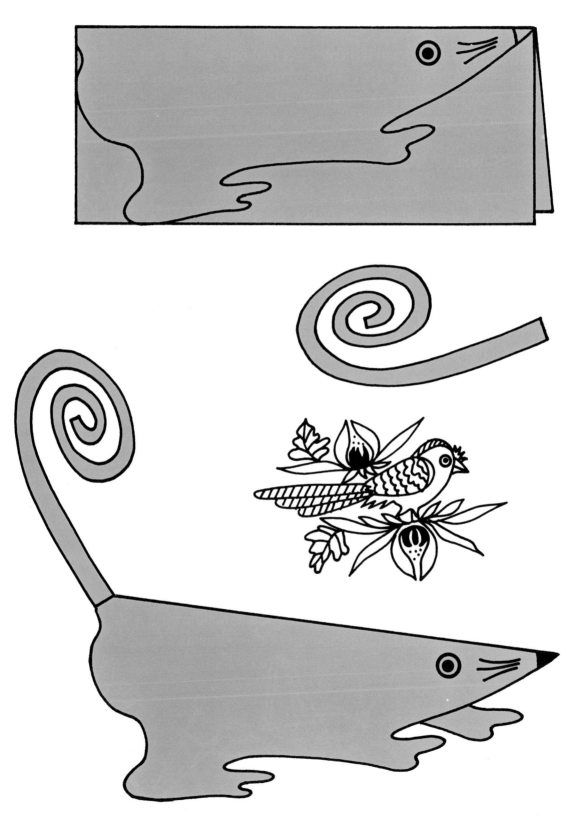

# Malaysian Mouse ●●●●●●●

This short, fat, simple mouse is like the ones carved out of wood in Malaysia. It might be fun to make a whole bunch of mice and arrange them on a table or on the floor. The mouse's plump shape is raised from a flat piece of folded paper.

## HERE'S WHAT YOU WILL NEED:

4" × 5" piece of gray construction paper, folded in half on the 5" side
pencil, scissors, brown felt-tip marker, glue
paper

## HERE'S HOW TO DO IT:

**1.** Fold the paper so that it measures 2" × 5". With the pencil, sketch the outline of the mouse onto the folded paper. Cut along the pencil line. Also cut along the edge that makes the mouse's ears. Unfold the mouse and make a cut down the length of his ears, to separate them. Now bend them slightly to give them a little more shape.

**2.** With the brown marker, draw the eyes and whiskers on each side of the mouse's face. Also color in his nose. To make the mouse's tail, cut a ¼" × 6" strip of paper. Roll one end around a pencil to curl it a bit. Glue the tail in place, as shown.

# Dragon Flag ●●●●●●●●●●●●

The dragon is one of the best-known Asian symbols. Throughout Asia there is much interest in and legend and folklore about dragons. They are used on many Asian arts and crafts. Dragons are thought to be both magical and powerful.

Bhutan is called the land of the dragon. Its modern-day flag has a dragon in the center of it. The thunder that is heard in the mountains is said to be the voice of the dragon.

The Chinese dragon stands for stability and endurance. A wingless reptile with a large head, long neck, and clawed feet, it is said to live in wonderful underwater palaces. As in Bhutan, dragons in China are thought to be responsible for thunder and lightning. The emperor's very special dragon has five claws; all other dragons have four. Yellow is the color of superior dragons. They are believed to bring the rain, and if offended, they can cause storms and flooding. We are going to make a Chinese dragon flag from about 1850.

## HERE'S WHAT YOU WILL NEED:

¼ yard of muslin, pencil, tracing paper,
    carbon paper, tape, glue
black fine-line felt-tip marker
yellow, red, and blue colored markers
3' long stick, or wooden dowel

## HERE'S HOW TO DO IT:

**1.** With the pencil, trace the pattern for the dragon onto the tracing paper. Cut the muslin, as shown.

**2.** Place the carbon paper on top of the muslin and tape it down. Now tape the tracing paper pattern onto the carbon paper to secure it. Draw over all the pencil lines again.

**3.** Remove the tracing paper, carbon paper, and tape from the muslin. Draw over the dragon with the black fine-line felt-tip marker.

**4.** Color the dragon yellow with blue eyes and a red tongue. Glue the flag to the top half of the stick, as shown. Now your dragon flag is ready to wave and enjoy.

# Indian Miniature Painting ● ● ●

Centuries ago, Indian artists began to create miniature paintings on the finest-quality handmade paper. They used paints that were made from natural minerals and vegetable and even animal pigments. These were prepared and made into paints according to formulas passed down from master to pupil.

Rich textures, with flat, vivid color, is the style of painting that developed in the eighteenth century. These miniatures had details painted in real gold. The one that you are going to make is of a fantastic, mythological bird (two choices are given), in a landscape of trees and flowers. The feathers on his head are golden, his front is full of glitter, and he has beautiful tail feathers.

Our miniature painting will also be made to look old by first "antiquing" the paper in a solution of coffee and water.

## HERE'S WHAT YOU WILL NEED:

1/4 cup instant coffee crystals
2 cups hot water in an 11″ × 13″ baking pan
several paper towels, teaspoon
8 1/2″ × 11″ piece of white paper
No. 2 soft lead pencil
tracing paper
black fine-line felt-tip marker
colored felt-tip markers
gold marker, glitter, glue

## HERE'S HOW TO DO IT:

**1.** Put the instant coffee in the baking pan and add the water. Stir until combined.

**2.** Gently put the paper in the solution and keep it there for half an hour.

**3.** Take out the paper, allowing the excess coffee to drip off. Place the paper between two paper towels and pat dry. Flatten it out and allow it to dry thoroughly.

**4.** Use the pencil to trace the designs onto the tracing paper.

**5.** Place the pencil-marked side of the tracing paper on top of the "antiqued" paper. Using the teaspoon, rub firmly along the pencil lines until all the designs are transferred.

**6.** Draw over all these pencil lines with the black fine-line felt-tip marker.

**7.** Color in the painting as you like with the other colored felt-tip markers.

**8.** With the gold marker, color in the feathers on the bird's head, a few in his tail, and some of the flowers.

**9.** Spread a little glitter on the front of the bird and then sprinkle a little glitter on top. Shake off the excess glitter. Now you have your finished Indian miniature.

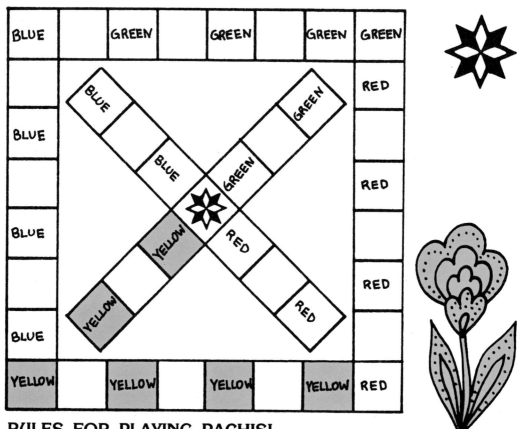

## RULES FOR PLAYING PACHISI

Pachisi is a game for two, three, or four players. Each player has one man, either yellow, red, blue, or green. The game is played with one large die, which is white on two sides and marked with yellow, red, blue, or green on the four remaining sides. The object of the game is to take each man on a complete trip around the game board and then up the diagonal strip from his home square to the center of the board.

The game begins with each player putting his or her man on the corner of the board that is the same color as the man. On the game board there are yellow, red, blue, and green corner squares.

One player throws the die until a colored side comes up; the player with the matching piece takes the first turn. He or she throws the die. If the die shows the same color as his or her piece, he or she may move his or her man one space in a counterclockwise direction and throw again. If the white side on the die turns up, the piece is not moved, but the player may throw again. If any other color appears on the die, the turn passes to the next player on the right.

The game continues this way until a player brings his or her man around the board and into the center. That player wins.

**44**

# Pachisi, An Indian Game ● ● ●

This is a very simplified version of Pachisi. Pachisi has been played in India since the seventeenth century and is still enjoyed today. This version is bright and colorful and fun to play.

## HERE'S WHAT YOU WILL NEED:

8″ square of white oaktag
1″ square of balsa wood, for die
black fine-line felt-tip marker
yellow, red, green, and blue felt-tip markers
pencil, ruler, saw
4 wooden clothespins that have a two-pronged opening, for men

## HERE'S HOW TO DO IT:

**1.** Using the pencil, draw a 1″ border all around the square of oaktag. Divide the border into 1″ squares, as shown.

**2.** Draw a 1″ cross in the middle of the square and divide it into smaller squares (seven on each side), as shown.

**3.** Now go over the pencil lines with the black felt-tip marker. Color in the squares, as shown. Draw a red star in the center square.

**4.** Ask an adult to help you with this part. And be very careful. To make the four playing pieces, or men, cut off the bottom of each of the clothespins with the saw. Check the illustration for this and for how to draw the faces on each man. Draw on the faces with the black felt-tip marker and color one in each of the four colors.

**5.** Color in the die with the felt-tip markers. Now begin to play your new game.

● ● ●                                                                ● ● ●

# Russian Sweet Treats ●●●●●

These buttery, sweet cookies are perfect for serving at a party or for a great snack. They travel well, so they could be packed easily for a school lunch.

## HERE'S WHAT YOU WILL NEED:

### Ingredients

1/2 cup sweet butter, softened
1/4 pound cream cheese, softened
1 cup flour
1/8 teaspoon salt
1/2 cup chopped walnuts
1/4 cup sugar
1 teaspoon cinnamon
extra flour

### Utensils

measuring cups and spoons
large mixing bowl
small mixing bowl
mixing spoon
dinner plate, aluminum foil
rolling pin, teaspoon
cutting board, knife
cookie sheet
pot holders

## HERE'S HOW TO DO IT:

**1.** Combine the butter and the cream cheese in the large mixing bowl. Stir until completely combined. Add the flour and salt. Mix well.

**2.** Shape the dough into seven balls. Put them on a dinner plate, cover with aluminum foil, and put into the refrigerator for several hours.

**3.** Ask an adult to help you with the baking. Heat the oven to 350°.

**4.** Lightly dust your cutting board with some of the extra flour. Now you will be rolling the balls into 6″ circles. Cut each circle into quarters.

**5.** In the small mixing bowl, combine the walnuts, sugar, and cinnamon. Drop a rounded teaspoon of this mixture onto each quarter of the dough.

**6.** To close the cookie up, pinch together the edges of the dough to form a half-moon shape, as shown. Place the cookies on an ungreased cookie sheet. Bake about 12 to 15 minutes, or until lightly browned. Makes twenty-eight cookies.

# Ghuryyebeh—Holiday Cookie from Lebanon

These delicious cookies have three slivered almonds decorating them and can be made in either a star or circle shape.

## HERE'S WHAT YOU WILL NEED:

### Ingredients

1 cup butter, softened
1 cup sugar
2 cups flour
extra flour for the cutting board
¼ pound whole almonds
extra butter to grease the
  cookie sheets

### Utensils

measuring cups and spoons
mixing bowl, spoon, cookie sheets
rolling pin, cutting board,
drinking glass, to cut cookies out
  with; cardboard, scissors, knife

## HERE'S HOW TO DO IT:

**1.** Put the butter and sugar in a large mixing bowl. Mix until light and fluffy. Add the flour, stirring until it is completely combined.

**2.** Sprinkle some of the extra flour onto the cutting board and roll out the dough to ⅓" thickness with the rolling pin. Cut out the dough with a glass whose open side has been dipped in some flour. Or you can copy onto the cardboard with a pencil the star pattern, and then cut it out. Then the cardboard pattern should be placed on the rolled dough and, with a knife, you can cut along the outside edge of the star.

**3.** Ask an adult to help you with the baking. Preheat the oven to 350°.

**4.** Place the cookies 1" apart on a greased cookie sheet. Decorate each cookie with an almond.

**5.** Bake the cookies in the oven for about 20 minutes, or until they are lightly browned along the edges. Makes about two dozen cookies.

# Index ●●●●●●●●●●●●●●●●●●